Moms e

ısule For

Motherho

ne years
f Workir
in 2012

ıding of
for their

dkar Un
my Ph.D
ook base

Delhi Pu

MPSEI

ce Co. L

ıve sacrıf

which ha
e affecte

ınd dinne

to assess

book, a
be happy
o strike a

f a wom
tands yo
mportant

:e in con
able off.

time. Ma

cipline i

n ideal v
  forecast:
;ood or u

usehold
narkable
ellent thi

those wł

n of L

' the Op
ık Sabha,
House (

ook narf

ıy by u
38, pavin

to earn
the freed
miliated

g.

ɔle modε

age life.

. While t
ıd husbaı
with a l

arria

of Divi

al, and s
ıgh life

f India

ιer than a

t societie

:est, mos
er have i

ss your e
nce with
ir minds.

ıd other :
healthy.

s is becau
ng and a

municat

ones, N(

distracte

pear to t
your par
your part

ves expi
d not sex

re than a
ul to apc

ole main
oser. If yo
artner, yo

you do n
intrudir

r, and ad

cus on tl
; you to]
to be ha

ren also
end wor

gious bo
e coming

's financ
critical t

ofessiona

aking

ecret ha

their pa

everyon

/alcohol

or nagge

ıacting (
suffered

al, and 1

ting to re

onfessio
insight ir

/een you
cial exp
oth cou

Marriage
alf denia

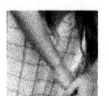

ɔpeɑ cɑp

the best

fter child
rized by
ı- depth

y be? *It*

ke a goal

taking d
tress.

and acc

of being

ı is to ta
ʍ chest

amount
help you

nilies an

, it is n

: the anir
repeat th

ourself a

er what y
from oth
you man

adults
and kids,

ꞁ help us
ꞁgth and ꞁ

;ivers/pai
ıge trust.

ırd when
people g

It is ess
rson ma
humilit

also has
increase

, free tir

stay calm
be home

o relax th
e one, ξ
partner

week if a
ed and
more in

writing
get read

nt.

f.

he procr

some t

t for gett

LY.

interest
resent" ν
divided -

attentior
choice,

mpse ab

:self and
neral op
t it is no

s and wa
)aths. Sh

1and to a

for enha
opic.

ou and
good hab

ome fear
f.

ome a ha

not all. J

s you ca

of expe

behavio
ions as e
mily car

a family

  Educati

ıpetent
face in li
ınd willii

ild to lov
his help

embers c
developi

iastic

away te

grandpar
it leads
hildren

onsider tl
ng a boc

ng and al
give up
randchil

˙S dysfur.

eedom t

The me
gger indi

I remain

d to the
rable to
their tota

use th
use and
ve and

tience. 1
a dysfun
. To ove

ite. Hav
al tightn

children

carrying

ouples n
it will be

s of heat
nely hot

ty issues
ion & sn

V.

n. Furth
pregnan
bies alik

ancy, th
iety that

leasant
' tell you
ılk to the

avyuha 1
r how to

; and are
the baby

baby bec
y of the

1.49kg

———

vegetabl

ied food.

ing abdo
.

abilities
 care of t
acts, phys

sis can c

y tempe
ısing the

NCY.

ᵉ of life.

ers & m

vith some

;e in tnos

ie with

)e remem

o go to
, playin

o, enjoy
a few m

WITH

have ma

equired,
is safe

vater ar

ders whi
l, clasp

o the list

gnancy]

aving, ba

the prese

)pen at w

r extra ti

hat exhil
dous wh
come fro

asks you
isor abo

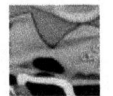

rom the
ecome a
lpless at

1).

bies usua

ıger, disc
s cries c
Regardl

Y (0-1 N

security

se when
positive

, and son
hungry (

ıl securıt
baby do
been dea

ie first v
nts must

tart show
:cognitio
their di

will hel

ake plac
of the b

or milk
ood sour
for you

ttention
s in a m

sonants]
/ voices (

vhile you

hear and

ıe on the

ing time
bies, unh

ıew baby

ome skil

ɔf the dev

grams to
gh calori

t of the

1 this sta

ıth to ex[

ds and si

s excited

onships l

baby me

:M SIGN

s down a
n 12 mor

ıuuıeıts.
ıired bef
ıt is norr

ains to m

ınd chart

ıge Skill

he leadi
groups.
e with a

for sl
, sit at tl

ler's curi
Γake ther

oddlers a

ings.

they on

travel fo
chedules

ιvailable

·k from h

l sharing
d caregiv

a loyal to
to take t
ne optic

ul time.

ime.

baby so

financia
en the ch
her goal

socio-e
ible num

and bab
of an athl

s reveal

childhood

s are a p
of 2 to 6
aking th

ᵇ or that v
ir book "
dren's eⁱ

, triangle

t alphabє
, body pa
and cap

vents an

tures and

ǀuires pɑ
ake spoɪ
do not kɪ

y with s
ı the tub
w with t

in each]

ence col
d various
elp the c

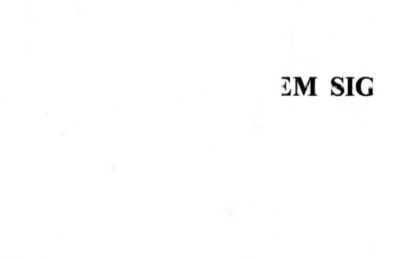

h a good

ttion that

ly envir

nd one-t
hich hel
prevent

reschool

e mornin

office.

and deve

lowship
gious fes
to the ch

nited tin
tunities t

es.

e must s

ions and
s to meet
.   .

ǝ. The p
iendship
ı. Siblinç

at differ
re are so
5vrs to 1

after the
appear.
oment sta

ls (Abov

ιe child

olving th
nethod v
er unders

ps, but s
with th
, althou

n

f.esteem

le child
school,
are diff

arning a
m. As th

c sense o

orders.

ating pat

uplift th
rison bu
ths and

ﺍﻳﻌﻌﭖ ﻟﻭ
ﻳﻪ challeı

oblem a
pect so t
if the b

thods to

1 like ch

ple may

ıg materi
; inquisit
e child a

all effo

ne and t
hing also
g people

en abov
and frie

her thar
enting, tl

·job by
r than try
you will
·

d abuse i
ms must

orking n
s which

home wl
unch bre

ble speci
nge the

nd play a
ption of
ȝ, etc. to

your fri
which v

ysical ch
l by hor
uberty be

: towards
g openl
.

nce to g
o meet tl
t physic

r gender
;ing time
that occu

ways of
h bound

t home,
ıde cook

. Peers c
eer press
ns or e

ad thei
obably n

an look
of life. A
they se

notions t
notional
d peer

ımon virt
ı-to-face.
ımunica

ss is pri

sly henc

loped the

soning, t

levelopm
take pla

es separ
lentity o
iscord o

)erstar in
activitie

ch hind

.d resear
ı differer

ɪust be ɑ

healthy

ɑ the ch

ɔr statii
hache. L
ɪy as hin

ith high
se so tha

ıd tears i
ı, and int

ık and na

es like ci

be a sigr
1.

are happ

Problen

nrontat

ghts (su

olescent
ents or s

sues.

rth desp

ιd ngure.

ιscious

ςtion, or

ords, stat
ol over
cave des

o build s

ve and
wanted n

ment wi
th profes
he help

berty the
food an
rinks. Th

re into s

v to iden

r-old fen
This also

eats and

hen all

to do w

)ed like
making

bility for
oose – an
 family i

hoice to

escents tl

indeper
lp for sl
a close r

ou care

re to say

vhat you

your cn

ns: Plar

l respons
its must
l to be in

nself/her

lf rather

ld is give

also val
ningful
mmunity

> their
ld, using

crotum, ᴏ

boundar

lt is a cri

blossom
onships

coercion

ner it is l

ng of foo

or becoi

;garding
; and Bo
set exp

one has
·obtrusiv
and bel

Technol

problem:
 Things
ed throu

and scho

sports e

ing your
ı can ad

ild a few
y? and s

ıdolescer

th diffic
feel cra

ot childi
she can
speaking

e and aft
the max
d and t

in the ca
) allows t
ild in a

avoid st
e. Make
tle, etc.,

cent and
ion whicl

d anxiety
and ot

w how th
w tips

and lapt
the chil

ks wheth
ust be re

positive
tified.

'one kno'

outings,

, focus o

she mus
ry to fin
in the far

ife and
er, who

or help f

rmation
vere writ

th a Do
rofessor
or Excel

her and
life. The

egnancy

ł conceiⱱ
s of her ր

kids be
th creativ

ıousehol
ne, Dr Pr

she ma
rning and

ıld not :
ve time.
but ofteı

nes, etc.
further to
i took tra

w-Autho

ent Profe

ishra is l

1 the e⟩
lreams. I
1g Wom⟨

Assistant
ogy (MA
kar worl

and pers
l gifts to

ııı. Aıth·
·otein an
ıich strer

r and m
he week
.   .

lorer's r
school s

a b a d

tain thi
ir parent

s. Jyoti h
ve them

I to leave
imes. Sl
rk and tl

of Ms Jy

sed that

life

rious a
e, inquis
e kids a

ative or
aking. H
rean as (

micable
he ritual
was sup

took to

fats and l

e prepare
nday so

che car
/s (who

he profe
. She en

ks, CDs,
ientific
i took ur

ne after t
ood morr

ores and
o tell her

cient, all
and ma
uresn as

lly upgra

, and pa

guidance

RPORA

DHYA P

vrs) is

language
dhir is a
the relat

ice of M
Pregnan

s and ex
ıd 2 hrs.
during t

f there v
t. She se
Abhiran

ive learr
g proble

urs to gi
for meal
a kiss a

ɔle but w
, educatiᴏ
s period

re suppo
gmental
ized and

ıg ın ho

·laws, lo·
academi
ʼn drean

e and Ba
unselor

coordina
age the c
ere were

d second
 yr of the
 wife was

Baby 1
and care
with th

lorer's r
:school s

..d t. .t.

Varun

ecking t
ldle scho

)mantic l

.s sought

upgrade

They wer
nowledg
rding ho

y life wi
happy t

gave an

G.Vajri

Prestig

8   yrs.),
itiatively

ly syster
uilt her ı
ing. Due

G. ADI

SHQA V

ty leave
her. On
ith maid.

ad indiff
ʒ mom,
ɔddlers s

ly. Adit
courage

ىeır steaₐ
helped tl
ingly thε

rofessior
-time ma

ıg & cy(
in the e
ional tuit

l confide
ınd   exp
ıe kids to

her pass
nd canno
ife, interi

) is a p
is a Ma
Nationa

cted acc
but stron
onship m

INI M. C

ice of M

ot the se
of the fir
ed her e

they had
ate for st

the mark

onal mot

rs. discu
rent new
gether in

study tir
school 1
1eir acti\

g to have
ner meal
akeover.

c. which
always.
r time fo

Women
Instituti
, IT & M

zational

. . . . . .

nary-car

יrg/resou

y.edu/art
themselv

Printed in the USA
CPSIA information can be obtained
at www.ICGtesting.com
LVHW021229210324
775007LV00001B/88

9 789356 683365